Life Lessons
from the
Dog

Amy Newmark

CSS

Chicken Soup for the Soul, LLC
Cos Cob, CT

Chicken Soup for the Soul: Life Lessons from the Dog
Amy Newmark

Published by Chicken Soup for the Soul, LLC www.chickensoup.com

Copyright ©2017 by Chicken Soup for the Soul, LLC. All Rights Reserved.

The publisher gratefully acknowledges the many publishers and individuals who granted Chicken Soup for the Soul permission to reprint the cited material.

Front cover and interior photo courtesy of iStockPhoto.com/GlobalP (© GlobalP).

Interior photo of Amy Newmark courtesy of Susan Morrow at SwickPix

Cover and Interior by Daniel Zaccari

ISBN: 978-1-61159-060-9

PRINTED IN THE UNITED STATES OF AMERICA
on acid∞free paper

25 24 23 22 21 20 19 18 17   01 02 03 04 05 06 07 08 09 10 11

Table of Contents

Seismic Lab

Labradors [are] lousy watchdogs. They
usually bark when there is a stranger about,
but it is an expression of unmitigated joy
at the chance to meet somebody
new, not a warning.
~Norman Strung

ur dog Dylan was a lousy watchdog. He was a large Lab mix and had the potential to be intimidating. But instead of barking when strangers came to the door, he'd greet them with an eager wag of his tail.

One night, my husband Craig left Dylan in our van parked by the ice arena where Craig was playing hockey. Dylan was happy hanging out in the van (he always jumped in as soon as we opened a door, never wanting to be left behind). And Craig figured the presence of a big dog would be a better deterrent to would-be thieves than a car alarm. When Craig came out of the arena near midnight, he was surprised to see Dylan running loose around the parking lot. It took Craig a moment to register that the van was gone. Not only had Dylan not deterred the car thieves, he must have happily jumped out of the van to greet them when they forced open a door (which was just as well, because we'd rather have lost the van than Dylan).

Despite Dylan's failing as a guard dog, we soon learned that he had the ability to raise an alarm of a different kind.

From the time we first adopted Dylan from a local animal shelter, he slept in a crate in our bedroom. When Dylan wasn't yet house-trained, we locked him in the crate at night. Later, we kept the door open and Dylan would head into the crate on his own as soon as Craig and I began preparing for bed. The crate became a place of sanctuary and security for Dylan. When anyone mentioned the word "bath," Dylan instantly hid in his crate. It was, therefore, out of character one night when Dylan refused to go into his crate. We pushed and coaxed, but he would not get inside. Instead, he slept on the floor at the foot of our bed. The next night was the same.

Coincidentally, shortly before this episode, I had been doing some research into the behaviour exhibited by animals before earthquakes. I had read that birds often stop singing moments before a quake hits and that dogs and cats have been known to avoid enclosed spaces (even to the point of running away from home) over a period of three days before an earthquake. On the third night that Dylan refused to go into his crate, I pointed out to my husband that Dylan might be displaying pre-earthquake behaviour.

"That would mean we should get an earthquake tomorrow," Craig said, half intrigued, half laughing.

We both went to sleep without giving it much further thought.

The next morning around 11:00 a.m., an earthquake hit. I was in the community centre swimming pool with my daughter at the time, and we didn't feel it. But the rest of the city did. It was a small quake, with no damage reported, but it did give people a bit of a scare. As one woman interviewed on the local news said, "It was like standing on Jell-O."

That night, Dylan returned to his normal pattern of happily bedding down in his crate, and Craig and I went to bed with a new feeling of security. Dylan might be a lousy watchdog when it came to burglars and car thieves, but when the next earthquake hits, we'll be ready.

~Jacqueline Pearce

Second Chances

*Go forward confidently, energetically
attacking problems, expecting
favorable outcomes.*
~Norman Vincent Peale

"**M**om, can we get a dog for Christmas?" my daughter Piper asked.

"We already have two dogs, honey."

"But she's so cute." Piper thrust her laptop screen in my face, and the dog's oversized gremlin-like ears elicited an "awww" from me.

Piper smiled, now hopeful.

"Well, I'll certainly give her cute," I admitted.

"But we can't handle another dog. Besides, getting a dog as a gift is never a good idea. It's impulsive. And most of those dogs…"

"I know, I know, end up in shelters." Piper knew the spiel from my previous dog rescue days. "But we'd never do that. Right?"

"That's right."

"I'll take care of her. I promise."

How many kids make that promise, only to ignore the dog once the novelty wears off? Wasn't that a common excuse for dumping dogs at the shelter? I raised my brows.

"Mom, I will. I promise." Piper pulled up a second photo of the red and white Corgi named Penny, and her stubby legs and soft brown eyes tugged at my heart.

I must resist, I reminded myself. I needed to identify a fault, so I scrutinized the picture. "Look." I pointed to her backside. "She doesn't have a tail."

"Mom, Pembroke Welsh Corgis don't have tails. That makes them even cuter." Piper flashed another photo of a Corgi lying frog-dog style with a full view of its thick-furred haunches. "They call their butts 'Corgi pants.' Isn't that funny?"

"Hilarious, but the answer's still no."

"The Queen of England has Corgis."

My affinity for all things British weakened my resolve. "Really?"

Piper said, "Yep."

Luckily, my sensibility immediately resurfaced. "No third dog. Period. End of discussion." I turned toward the kitchen to prepare dinner.

"Penny's a rescue."

She had to go and say the "R" word. I sighed. Piper could sense I was softening, so she brought it on home. "Mom, doesn't every dog deserve a second chance?"

As an advocate for shelter dogs, how many times had I said those same words? "Yes, they do. But it will have to be someone else who gives it to her. We have our hands full with Frodo and Dexter. It wouldn't be fair to Penny." Did I really believe that? She'd have knowledgeable and responsible dog owners, an established pack family, and a loving forever home. What was my real hangup?

Piper sulked in her chair throughout dinner. She had talked about becoming a vet or a dog trainer. Maybe Penny was just what she needed: a dog of her own.

After dinner, I went into my office to work, but I was moved by Penny's plight—her heartbreaking story unfolded on the Internet. A puppy mill survivor, she was terrified of noises, daily activity, and people. She'd require much patience and training. I recalled my days in Greyhound rescue—fostering the abused and neglected ex-racers—and the miracles that had occurred with consistency, gentleness, and love. Why had I stopped fostering anyway? Time? No. Effort? No. Burnout? Yes. I'd simply lost faith in mankind, and the sadness had overwhelmed me.

As Christmas neared, Piper no longer mentioned Penny, but she didn't have to. The little dog still needed a home for the holidays, and I knew we could provide the love and understanding she'd need to recover from her past trauma. But was I ready to jump into such an emotional commitment again? After much reflection, I decided to apply for her adoption and surprise Piper if our application was accepted. We interviewed with Linda, the founder of the adoption group, and she believed us to be a good match for Penny. Dexter and Frodo accepted her into their pack without incident during the mandatory home visit. A few days later, Penny had a new home for the holiday.

Spending the first few months in various hidey-holes throughout our house, Penny slinked into the kitchen for meals, only to retreat back into the darkness. She ducked her head and crouched whenever we reached to pet her. At times, we sat in the closet entryway, speaking her name softly and reassuringly, hoping to gain her trust. We allowed her to set the parameters of our interaction: how much and how long. The phrase "Where's Penny?" became our household mantra. While I pulled Penny out of the nooks and crannies of our home to take her outside each evening, Penny pulled me deeper into the world of Corgi rescue. Hundreds of dogs like Penny hid out of fear, and I could no longer hide from my duty to help them.

It started slowly with monetary donations, attending adoption affairs, such as meet-and-greets, and supporting Corgi fundraising events. We connected with the Corgi rescue folks, and Penny started to flourish after Piper enrolled her in obedience training and agility. As our love for Penny grew, and we witnessed her healing, I knew I had to offer more. As a professional writer, I had a skill the group could utilize. I'd help to become the voice of those who couldn't speak. I began by writing the text for the rescue's new website. The factual information wasn't sad: the application process, tips on feeding and grooming, agility opportunities, the various dogs available for adoption. I can do this, I thought.

"Would you be willing to write the dogs' bios for our annual calendar?" Linda soon asked me.

Wait. Bios would require telling the dogs' stories, their disturbing histories with the sordid facts of their abuse and neglect before they came into rescue. Facts that I didn't want to hear, stories I didn't have the strength to tell. But how could I say no? It was my chance to give back to the rescue for the love and joy that Penny had brought into our family.

Linda provided me with the heartrending details of the rescued dogs, and I wept as I read of their mistreatment: broken bones, soft tissue damage, heartworm disease, fleas, severe anxiety, and malnutrition to name a few. There was Sydney, once abandoned, frightened, obese, and suffering from severe tooth decay, who became an AKC Canine Good Citizen and now visits libraries during children's story hour. And Finley, struck by two cars while living on the streets, who now chases rabbits in his back yard and provides love to his adoptive family. Grits spent the first fourteen months of his life in a crate because his family had no time for him but, once in rescue, earned his Master Agility

Champion title and the myriad accolades that followed because Linda saw promise in his athleticism and intelligence. As I spun each dog's yarn for others to read, the Corgis' mental and physical scars were swiftly counterbalanced by their successes. These dogs had been offered a second chance, and I marveled at their adaptability and fortitude.

Today, their histories of cruelty and neglect no longer make me cry. Each year, as the calendar season commences, I sit down to the gut-wrenching facts and craft stories of hope that offer people a glimpse into the dogs' strength and perseverance—the miracle of dog rescue. And, just like Penny, I've been given a second chance.

~Cathi LaMarche

Gift of the Shepherd

*Mirth can be a major tool for insight,
changing "ha-ha" to "aha."*
~Author Unknown

As I completed one holiday chore after another, my neck and shoulders began to ache from stress. I heard music drifting out of every store at the mall. A male voice crooned "chestnuts roasting on an open fire…" The holiday spirit filled my heart, but my body needed a hot soak in the tub.

My fingertips read the Braille list that I pulled from my pocket. I visualized mountainous displays of clothes and toys to our left and right. With my guide dog Misty leading the way, the mall madness did seem a bit more manageable. Still, shoppers asked if they could pet my German Shepherd, even though her harness sign read, "Please do not pet me. I'm working." She eased me between the crowds, while I imagined their outstretched hands. Finally, my list grew shorter as the bags grew heavier.

Back home, some chores disappeared from the list while new chores were added. My husband Don and I had decorated our tree. The lights and ornaments were spaced perfectly—no "Charlie Brown" tree for us. Why were we so obsessed with our decorations? We dressed the tree as though Martha Stewart would stop by. Don and I had wrapped the presents and placed them beneath the tree. For each purchase, we had gone over budget, hoping we chose just the right gift.

The next day, ingredients lined our kitchen counter for cookie baking. My guide dog flitted at my feet. Normally, at this time of day, we would be returning from our daily walk. Then she loved being brushed. But her grooming routine needed to wait along with a walk. Once again, I felt her cold nose nuzzle my skirt, so my floured hand waved her away. She brought in her favorite toy and dropped it. I tossed the rubber ring into the next room to keep her out of the kitchen. Who wants dog hair in their cookies? Within minutes, cinnamon and vanilla perfumed our kitchen. I pulled out the first tray of cookies and turned to put them on the table. Our cookie baking reminded me of a factory. My husband, without hesitation, had the next batch going into the oven. The kitchen mess reminded me that we still didn't have any time to relax.

A bunch of stamped Christmas cards sat on the table. I still needed to Braille a message in each card sent to blind friends. Would I have the time or energy?

"After this last batch of cookies, I'm going to play with her," I told Don. Suddenly, I could not ignore a loud sound nearby. "Crunch!" Misty had swiped a cookie off the cooling tray. I used a firm tone of voice: "No." The success of our partnership depended on praise and gentle correction from me. Like a child's cry for attention, Misty's mischievous behavior announced her boredom. A few minutes later, I felt guilty for ignoring her. "Here's a biscuit, girl," I said, using the treat as a peace offering instead of praise.

Then, Misty was oddly absent from the kitchen, after being underfoot all morning. I searched the house. When I called her name, I followed the sound of her thumping tail. Her body stretched full-length beneath the Christmas tree. As I reached to pet her, my hand felt her dog biscuit. Misty had placed her treat in the manger scene next to the figurine of the Christ child. For the first time that day, I laughed.

Misty's gift to me fit perfectly, was suitable for my age, the price was just right, and I did not have to exchange it. Misty reminded me to "stop and smell the pine boughs." The blessing of the season,

I learned from my furry pal, is sharing time with those we love.

~Carol Chiodo Fleischman

The Taxi Stops Here

You don't learn to walk by following rules.
You learn by doing, and by falling over.
~Richard Branson

ikki was my third child. She was a beautiful, blond little angel. Anita was four and Michelle five, and I worried about jealousy when this new baby entered our lives. Lucky for me, the only jealousy was about who got to play with her and help care for her.

My other worry was that we had two dogs and two cats, all of which had joined our family after our daughters were well past the baby stage. The pups had grown into two majestic Collies, and the cats? Well, they were just two ordinary cats. Johnny was a small black and white cat, and Ringo was a huge gray and black striped tabby.

The old Collie I grew up with lived long enough to help raise our first two baby girls, but had passed away. I was pretty confident that my new Collies would work out well too. But I'd never had a cat around a newborn baby. I worried about one climbing into the crib or accidentally scratching her. As soon as we brought Nikki home, we saw this was not going to be a problem because the two Collies would not allow either cat to get close to the baby. One or both stayed on guard next to her 24/7. If I was nursing her, bathing her or dressing her, one of the dogs would be right there. At night, our golden sable Collie, Windsong, slept by her cradle, and later under her crib. Tiffany, our black and gold tricolor, slept on the round throw rug, blocking the doorway to the bedroom. Any cat venturing near got a growl and a quick snap.

Nikki was a bright, energetic and happy baby

who seemed to learn a new capability every day, but by the time she was nine months old, she had not yet tried to take a step on her own. She crawled like a speed demon everywhere.

She did pull herself up to stand by the couch or bed. But despite our outstretched arms, she would immediately drop to her hands and knees and crawl to us. While no parent wants to compare children, at times it's hard not to. Michelle had been up and walking at nine months, Anita by ten months. I had photos of each taking their first steps. Nine months came and went. Then ten became eleven. Nikki was not walking. I took her to our pediatrician in a panic. What was wrong with my baby girl? She was almost a year old, and she not only did not walk, she refused to even try.

The doctor checked her and found absolutely nothing wrong. He assured me that all children walk at different times and that she would walk when she was ready. If she wasn't walking after she turned a year old, he would run more tests.

That evening I discussed my fears with my husband. Nikki was in the playroom with Anita and her ever-present Collie nursemaids. Michelle was sprawled on the kitchen floor with her crayons and a coloring book. My husband was trying to reassure me that the doctor was right. Nikki would walk when she was ready.

"Why should she walk when she has the taxi?" Michelle piped up, not even looking up from her coloring book.

"What do you mean, taxi?" her father asked.

Michelle explained that when they were alone playing in the playroom and Nikki wanted to get from one point to another, she just grabbed onto the two Collies and lifted her legs and the dogs simply carried her wherever she wanted to go.

"I've never seen this," I said. "I'm with her all the time."

"Mommy," Michelle said, "Nita an' me watch her too, when you're busy. She does it all the time."

"Why didn't you tell me?" I asked.

"You never asked," she said solemnly. "Bet she's doin' it right now."

My husband and I exchanged glances, then quietly went down the hall to the playroom. We went to the door, which was blocked with a security gate. I gasped in amazement. The two Collies were trotting in a circle all around the room. Nikki was between the two dogs, her little fists clutching tightly to each dog's thick ruff. She had her legs tucked up high and was giggling with delight as the two Collies took her around and around the room. Anita was playing with a doll, paying no attention to Nikki and the dogs.

I cleared my throat loudly. Nikki immediately let go of the dogs and dropped onto all fours and scuttled across the room to the door, where she sat holding her arms up to me to be picked up.

The next day was awful. We took the dogs away from Nikki and put them in the back yard. The first hours were full of Nikki throwing the first tantrums of her young life. Everyone ignored her except for tempting her to walk with favorite toys or cookies. In response to the ruckus Nikki was making, the Collies barked, whined, scratched at the back door and, as a last resort, started howling like wolves separated from their cub. Michelle and Anita went out to soothe the dogs.

After about four hours, Nikki got tired of being ignored and pulled herself up to her feet. To cheers and encouragement from her sisters, she toddled across the room to get a cookie I was holding out as a bribe. When my husband came home from work that evening, she toddled to the door to greet him. He lifted her high in the air and then hugged her.

The next day, I let Windsong and Tiffany back in, but watched them closely to make sure there were no further "taxi" incidents. They went to Nikki and kissed her all over. She showed off for them, walking all around the room. They seemed to know automatically that they were no longer needed for transportation. Windsong went back to sleeping by my bed at night, while Tiffany took on the full nanny burden. If Nikki got close to anything that might hurt her, the big black Collie was there in a flash, herding her back to safety and maybe hoping that Nikki would want a lift. But Nikki never hitched a ride again. The doggy taxi was definitely out of business.

~Joyce Laird

Six Pounds of Therapy

With the past, I have nothing to do;
nor with the future. I live now.
~Ralph Waldo Emerson

t was the most difficult year of my life. My grown daughter had been diagnosed with a rare tumor that would require radiation and chemotherapy, followed by surgery. A beautiful, loving, smart and active young woman, she had a good job and was finally living the life she wanted. But in a flash her life had changed, and so had mine.

I'm the kind of mother who has always felt my

children's pain deeply and I swore I'd always be strong for them when life threw them a curveball and they needed me to be their rock. But the seriousness of my daughter's affliction shattered my heart and sent me in a downward spiral into depression. It was unfamiliar territory and I struggled against it with everything I had. There was no way I'd let her see what was happening to me; she had enough on her plate. But the black vortex kept sucking me down.

That summer my fourteen-year-old dog and best friend, Allie, came to the end of her journey and I had to make the painful decision of letting her go. She had bladder cancer, but with medication and diapers she hung on for a year. Now she had renal failure too and her tired body was giving up the fight. Allie and I shared laughter, triumphs and tragedies and she was always by my side. She always understood me. Now I had to go on without her and I didn't know how I was going to do that. Losing her was another major blow. I was consumed with grief and spiraled downward even faster.

By September I'd reached the lowest point of my entire life. It was the first time I felt out of control and I didn't know what to do. I barely ate, couldn't sleep and spent hours a day crying. My anxiety level was through the roof and there were times I could barely breathe. I had no choice but to visit my family doctor to see if she could prescribe something that would help lift me out of this darkness.

I'd never been one to take prescription medicine, except antibiotics when I needed them. Heck, I rarely even took over-the-counter medicine! So I was nervous about taking a drug to calm my anxiety, and my stomach was in knots. I put the unopened prescription in my bag and kept trying to get a handle on things without it.

About a week later my sister suggested that I think about rescuing a little dog. She told me I was the kind of woman who needed to nurture. Taking care of a dog in need of a good home might just be the answer for me.

At first I thought the idea of bringing another

dog into my life at this time would be nuts. But the more I thought about it the more I realised I really was born to nurture; it made me feel complete. Maybe I would give it a shot.

My sister found two-year-old Ziggy through a local pet network. The ad said he'd been spending most of his days alone and his owner came to the decision the little guy deserved a loving forever home with someone who had time for him.

The moment I laid eyes on little Ziggy, my heart belonged to him.

A six-pound Chihuahua mix with a small bearded face, soft brown eyes and a tiny body with a thick layer of black hair on his back and practically none on his legs and under side, he was completely adorable.

Ziggy came home with me and I quickly discovered he was the best therapy I could have asked for. He taught me to focus on one moment at a time. With every passing day, life got brighter. Before long I was sleeping like a rock, my appetite had picked up and the knot in my stomach was gone.

Ziggy has shown me how to live in the moment. He is a little clown and his antics are hilarious. He's also a great inspiration and a wonderful little snuggler when I need to hold him or he needs me close. He depends on me and I lean on him and together we make a great team.

My troubles are still there but I'm not looking at things the way I did for the past year. Now I'm able to accept the fact I can't change what's happened to my daughter and I can't fix it. All I can do is love her with all my heart and pray she's going to be okay.

Of course I still miss my precious Allie, but now I focus on the happy times we shared before she got sick. I know I did everything I could for her and gave her a happy life filled with love.

Little Ziggy is a superhero in my eyes, because I'm a giant compared to him and yet he's able to carry me with no effort at all. He keeps me smiling. And when I look into those soft brown eyes, I can see the promise of tomorrow and the happiness of today. He is love and loyalty all bundled up in a cute, energetic little body.

P.S. I never did open that prescription bottle.

~Annabel Sheila

That Dog Can't Walk

The difference between perseverance and
obstinacy is that one comes from a strong will,
and the other from a strong won't.
~Henry Ward Beecher

The last thing we needed was another animal in the house. We had enough discord between the two cats and Hoss, our very naughty Dachshund. But Pumpkin was an abandoned puppy, and my daughter Alice adopted her. It was crazy to allow yet another dog into our household, but I guess I'm crazy.

"We're going to call her Pumpkin because it's almost Halloween," the kids informed me at dinner. "She even looks like a Pumpkin. Look how round she is, and her brown patches are sort of orange."

I took Pumpkin to Dr. Genet, our veterinarian, for a checkup. She greeted the vet with a happy face and wagging tail. You'd think he was her very best friend. She showed interest in everything he was saying. "She's a very young pup and healthy, but an unusual mix of breeds," the vet said. "Collie head, Basset Hound body, Dachshund feet. The tail is King Charles Spaniel." She was quite a funny looking dog.

None of it mattered. What mattered was that we had the happiest animal I ever met. She was delighted to join our menagerie, watching and imitating the other animals, eager to fit in. At first, we wondered if her vocal cords were impaired. She never barked. But after listening to our noisy cats and our other dog, she attempted to join in the racket. What came out of her sounded like a mix of meow and woof, as though she wasn't sure which language was hers.

When Hoss challenged the cats, Pumpkin pranced about behind him, imitating his dance, learning to be a dog. Pumpkin watched and learned from Hoss, but unlike Hoss, she had a dose of common sense. She'd join him in annoying the cats, but only to a point. She'd help chase them and bark at them, but never mimicked any of the more stupid moves that earned him many a scratched and bloodied snout.

As Pumpkin aged, she grew plumper and plumper and began to resemble an overinflated balloon with a head and tail. People often laughed at the sight of her. "What kind of dog is that?" they'd ask. Listing all of her breeds took too long, so my son created a shortcut. "She's a hippo spaniel," he'd say and folks would look more closely. "Interesting. I don't know the breed," they'd mumble, and walk away.

Then Pumpkin developed a problem. It showed up one evening when she couldn't move her hindquarters. My husband took her to the vet on his way to work the next morning. When I finished teaching that day, I met with Dr. Genet for his diagnosis. The news was not good. "That heavy Basset body on that elongated Dachshund spine is the problem," he said. Tests, X-rays and other imaging techniques indicated surgery.

When, after her treatment, I went to take Pumpkin home, the news was still grim. The veterinarian said they had done what they could, and there was a sixty percent chance she might recover the use of one leg. But in the meantime, to help the healing, Pumpkin needed to be confined. He brought out parts of a large cage for me to take home and assemble.

I carried Pumpkin to the car and put her in the seat next to me. She rested her chin on my lap and looked up at me with her glad-to-see-you smile. My heavy heart was lightened by her happy spirit. I stroked her head and smiled back.

The kids refused to construct the cage as I'd asked. I explained again its importance for Pumpkin's recovery. They insisted that her being free, where they could hug and hold her and let her know she was loved, was more important than the maybe recovery of some movement to one leg. I relented and Pumpkin remained uncaged.

It upset me to see her dragging her still paralyzed back parts this way and that behind the dancing Hoss, who was busy threatening the cats. My attempts to keep Pumpkin still were unsuccessful. She was so happy being back in the game. She dragged along, adding her meow-bark to the noise and grinning. I let her be.

By the end of the first week, she was pushing valiantly with her right leg, over and over again, trying to make it hold her up. It was hard to watch. Didn't she know it was hopeless?

By the second week, though, I had to wonder. Each day, she was up on her right rear leg for longer and longer stretches, with the left one now making pushing movements as well. She made progress daily.

A month passed and it was time for Pumpkin's post-op visit to the vet. My husband dropped her off on his way to the office and I went to get her after work. When they brought Pumpkin out, she dashed over to greet me. I leaned down to attach her leash.

"Don't go," the receptionist said. "The doctor needs to see you." My heart sank. I sat down, dreading more bad news. I should have kept her in the cage, I thought. The vet came out and indicated I should follow him into the examining room. Pumpkin trotted along beside me, grinning up at Dr. Genet, her tail wagging.

He had a pair of X-ray films hanging. Pointing along the first one as he spoke, Dr. Genet explained in detail the anatomy of a normal dog's spinal column. I felt like I was back in biology class.

He moved to the second frame. "Now this is the X-ray of Pumpkin's back," he said, pointing at the spinal cord. Remember what I told you about the importance of this for movement?" I nodded. "Now see where this disc has penetrated into the spinal cord here, practically severing it?" I nodded again. Dr. Genet turned his attention to Pumpkin, still prancing happily about the room, uninterested in his lecture. He pointed directly at her. "That dog cannot walk," he announced firmly.

He sounded almost angry with her. "I'm sorry," I said, "but she had cats to chase." Dr. Genet shook his head and laughed. "Motivation is powerful medicine. It's one of science's greatest mysteries. Like love." Then he leaned down and petted Pumpkin's head. "Good girl," he said. "Good girl."

~Marcia Rudoff

Blend Well

*There is no psychiatrist in the world
like a puppy licking your face.*
~Ben Williams

"Let's get a dog," I said. Scott looked at the picture of a one-pound, one-ounce little white ball of fur with big black eyes looking back at him from my computer screen.

The next day we were in the car "just to look."

As the woman walked out with the tiny white ball of puppy, my heart melted. I immediately reached for him. I don't remember talking about it. I just remember thinking "he's ours now." I looked at my smiling husband and knew he felt the same. I handed the puppy to Scott while I fumbled to prepare the car for our new addition.

Scott held our new baby, well, like a new baby. He stood perfectly still and upright. Fear on his face. He didn't even talk. I'm not even sure he was breathing. I grabbed the puppy back from a now relieved looking Scott and we headed home.

The ride home was filled with phone calls and announcements.

"We got a puppy!"

After the flood of calls the conversation turned to logistics. What would he eat? Where would he sleep? What would we call him? Barney. We will call our newest little family member Barney. A name cleverly thought up by my mother-in-law.

Scott and I had married only three months earlier and had become a ready-made-family. He had two boys; I had one boy. We struggled to learn our roles with our new family members. Blending a family is not easy and not instant. We had different rules, different ways of life, and we needed to find common ground.

Scott and I decided to surprise the boys with the new puppy. Each boy, one by one, entered the room, smiled, and fell to the floor to get closer to our new addition.

"Who is this?"

"Did we get a dog?"

"Can we play with him?"

"He's so small."

We all fell silent as Barney took his tiny first steps over to investigate a new brother waiting across the room. As he reached his destination we all laughed and beamed with pride. I scanned the room and noticed all eyes were on Barney. The boys were laughing and calling out for him. They joked with each other and us about the tiny dog. Could Barney be the answer? Could it be this little dog could somehow bring us together?

We all watched as Barney learned his name, learned to go outside, and finally learned how much he loved treats. Eventually the little one-pounder grew to a hefty six pounds. He was still so small. But he had a giant personality. No matter what the mood of the house, Barney would change it. At any moment he would trot into a room and look at us like he was saying, "What are we doing, guys?" Everyone would smile. He had the ability to make a bad situation good or a good situation better. But most of the time he would just show up. He wouldn't expect anything. He just wanted to be a part of whatever was going on.

He didn't know he was part of a blended family. He just knew we were his family. He didn't love one more than another. He didn't see a stepbrother or stepparent. He just saw a family—his family. Barney became more than common ground for the family. For me, he became an example of how I want to live my own life.

Fill the room with unconditional love, show up, and bring treats.

~Diana Lynn

Wayward Setter

Thorns may hurt you, men desert you,
sunlight turn to fog; but you're never
friendless ever, if you have a dog.
~Douglas Mallock

After many years of being without a dog, and at my daughter's request, I scanned the newspaper looking for one. I had raised Irish Setters for many years, so I thought that another one would fill the empty spot in our lives. I also was married at the time to a man who never seemed to take any joy in anything that I did. Surely, I thought, another Setter would bring him to his senses. In my mind, he'd be so happy that I came up with the idea, this would certainly bring the happiness back into our marriage!

I saw an ad for an English Setter from a breeder not two miles away! I knew it! This was meant to be. My daughter and I picked out an adorable puppy that was all white, except for an endearing spot of brown around one eye. Taking the wriggly pup home, we waited for my husband's approval.

Unfortunately, we were met with disapproval. Despite my best training efforts, in his eyes the puppy could do nothing right. He chewed on shoes; he jumped on furniture; he howled when left alone. Despite crate training, several long walks per day, as well as obedience training, Patrick, as we called him, was a very wayward Setter. I could handle the puppy being, well, a puppy, but what I couldn't handle was my husband's growing discontent and his conversations that began and ended with, "Get rid of THAT dog!"

My daughter was beside herself. She too had tried, but Patrick weighed fifty pounds now and he still hadn't turned into the beloved family member we had hoped. The strain on the family was ridiculous!

Then, one after another, small miracles happened. My daughter, out of the blue one day, inquired, "Mom, why don't you write a book about Patrick?"

I chuckled. "A book? Why would I write a book about Patrick? What would I say?"

She knew that I had been doing small writing jobs, but never anything big and certainly not a book. My inner fear took over. Who would want to read a book about a wayward Setter anyway? Hmm, a wayward Setter…

I sat at the computer, pulled up a blank page, and began: "Patrick was born one fine day in January, just before the coldest weather set in…." I kept writing until I had what I thought was a good, rough draft of chapter one. My daughter eagerly read it. "Yup, this is good! Now, keep going!"

Again I chuckled. Only twelve years old, she had such faith in me… and in our puppy.

Two weeks later, while gathered at a Fourth of

July fireworks show, we discussed the plot of the story. Curious, my husband asked what we were talking about.

"The book that Mom is writing. It's about Patrick!" she said.

"Hmmph! Your mom can't write a book!" His lack of faith in me was so disappointing.

"She is too, and it's going to make money and then you'll see just how valuable that dog is to us!" she exclaimed.

"I doubt it. He's just a dumb dog that you just HAD to have!"

I looked at my daughter—her crestfallen face said enough. That was all the motivation that I needed. I said no more about it to him, but used every chance I had in between my jobs and caring for my kids to write. Early mornings turned into late nights, then, finally, I submitted the idea to several publishers. Within three weeks, one wrote back, asking to see my manuscript, which I sent in. The response made me cheer! It was accepted! *Patrick the Wayward Setter* would be published within nine months!

It was followed by three sequels. As I gained a following of readers, more ideas for book submissions came. Soon I was writing Western fiction, then non-fiction books. My marriage, however, took the hit. My husband, jealous of the attention, decided that I needed to make a choice: my writing or him. Our marriage had not been anything more than a piece of paper for many years. I made my choice.

In 2012, at age nine, Patrick's health took a turn for the worse. This dog, whose loyalty was proven through my book signings, where he sat patiently as readers oohed and aahed over this canine hero of stories, who saw me through a difficult divorce and the aftereffects of rebuilding my life, was now leaving me. I was heartbroken. How does one repay a dog's devotion? I stayed with him until the very end. When the injection put him to sleep for the last time, I finally broke down.

Today, I look back at how much this dog influenced my life. If not for Patrick, I would never have had the courage to write, not professionally anyway. I would not have had the chance to meet so many people who have told me what a difference my words have made in their lives. It was through this animal that I found the courage to leave a sad relationship and to love again.

~Diane Ganzer Baum

Gentle Giant

I think dogs are the most amazing creatures;
they give unconditional love. For me they are
the role model for being alive.
~Gilda Radner

When we got to the shelter that day, my husband, son, and I split up in our quest to find the perfect dog. Eight months before we had lost our Bogey. We finally felt ready to open our hearts and home again, opting for an older pet.

I checked each cage, my heart constricting with emotion. Dog after hopeful dog approached, tail wagging, trusting eyes begging me to take it home.

As I approached the last cage, a massive dog stood up and wandered over. His sad, penetrating gaze captured mine and I couldn't look away. I extended my hand. He leaned forward to smell it politely, his enormous tail wagging slowly. Everything about him seemed to say, "You don't want me either, do you?"

When I read the tag hanging from his enclosure, I gasped. He'd been at the shelter for six of his eighteen months!

"This one!" I yelled out to my family, startling a young couple.

"He's gigantic," my husband declared.

"He must weigh a hundred pounds," my son added.

"One-twenty," I corrected, tapping the tag. "But I still want him." I was surprised when they both agreed.

As we led him outside, he blinked in the bright daylight, inhaling the fresh air with inquisitive, huffing snorts. We saw that his extended confinement hampered his motor skills and development. He stared blankly at the open car door, not knowing what was expected of him. We tried to coax him to jump in, but he simply stood there, uncertain and confused. We finally had to lift him into the vehicle, where he buried his mighty head into my son's lap, lying rigid with fear for the entire ride home.

The poor creature seemed even more mystified by the three steps leading to the house, needing encouragement, guidance, and soft tugs on his collar to climb them. Inside, he barely explored his new surroundings. Spotting the staircase balusters that led to the basement, he plopped down against them. A cage was all he'd known for half a year, and, recognizing bars, he gravitated to the familiar.

We named him Jack, and for the next eleven years, we were blessed to know this gentle giant. He eventually learned to take stairs, but not gracefully. He could descend easily, but going up was an entirely different matter. He would need to gather momentum from a running start clear across the yard. Occasionally, he miscalculated his speed or the distance between steps, but he persevered, repeating his process tirelessly until he succeeded. His determination was a reminder that nothing comes easy—that all goals have obstacles and require patience to achieve.

Despite his intimidating size, few people feared Jack. He emitted an aura of peaceful serenity. He'd give a warning "smile" and a low rumble that could shake the ground if he felt his "people" were at risk, but his motto seemed to be "Do no harm unless threatened."

We would watch, amazed, as he lay in the back yard surrounded by birds, some pecking at the breadcrumbs we provided, others actually daring to land on his back before flying away unharmed. Squirrels scampered by without trepidation. His only reaction was to raise his colossal head and stare at them quizzically before resuming his nap. His tolerant behavior made me rethink killing bugs, if they were merely going about their insect business.

Jack expected nothing from us. He loved

unconditionally and was content with any attention or food offered. He was simply grateful to be a part of our lives, and to move freely in our home and on our property. Each time we let him out, he stopped and sniffed at the air appreciatively as if he couldn't believe that he was free.

Huge as he was in size, the biggest part of him was the heart that stored so much love, loyalty and perception. He instinctively knew when to move out of the way to avoid collision, just as he sensed the right time to lean against any of us in comfort and quiet reassurance through difficult times.

Jack was almost thirteen when his time with us began to come to an end. One morning, I found him on the kitchen floor unable to move. I'd owned enough dogs to recognize a stroke. There was little I could do except make him comfortable. Our veterinarian confirmed that.

I remained vigilant for signs of pain or discomfort, knowing Jack would tell me in that way only dogs can when it was time. For three days, I never left his side, feeding him if he wanted it, offering water as needed, and cleaning him tenderly when necessary. I would lie beside him, whispering that it was okay to leave us, yet he continued to cling to life, ever loyal, ever concerned for our sadness. On the third morning, I woke up to find him sitting up weakly, wagging his tail. Seeing I was awake, he slumped down and our eyes locked, giving me the heartbreaking message I had been waiting for.

We carefully moved him to our van for his final ride. We gave him a moment to look around his home and property for the last time before sliding the door shut. As we drove, I lifted his limp head to feel the breeze and watch the passing cars.

When we got to the vet's, we transferred him to the waiting gurney. I tried to still my shaking body and muffle my sobs, but was unable to, not then—not during the time the attendants compassionately allowed us to say goodbye.

We surrounded him and held him as he slipped away. Jack's last lesson to us was to accept death with courageous dignity. For a nanosecond before his beautiful eyes closed forever, I saw a glimpse of his former strength and spirit, almost as if he was anticipating this new journey with renewed youth. His tail swished one last time as he sagged into my arms, and I saturated his thick fur with my tears.

When we left him that day, there was no pro-found sign that he was okay. No rainbow split the sky, no sunbeams broke through clouds, but I wasn't surprised. Jack taught me that every day of freedom to breathe fresh air and marvel at the sights around us was a gift, one he never took for granted and embraced with heartfelt gratitude and appreciation.

~Marya Morin

Doggy-Nanny

Biology is the least of what
makes someone a mother.
~Oprah Winfrey

When my family and I realized that our Golden Labrador, Gypsy, was going to have puppies, we were excited. After all, these would be the first puppies born on our property in well over ten years. But at the same time, a voice in my head said, "Brace yourself."

As cute as puppies are, they are a lot of work, and the circumstances were far from ideal. To begin with, Gypsy was around ten years old when a certain white German Shepherd came to visit, and she never had been known as the "sharpest tool in the shed." My parents knew from experience that Labradors had large litters of puppies. And given Gypsy's age and the risk of the birthing process, we had no doubt we would be doing more than our fair share of raising the little darlings until they were old enough to place in good homes. We needed help, but where is a nanny when you need one? Enter the doggy-nanny!

Her name was actually Freebie. She was a German Shepherd that a veterinarian had given us when our beloved Collie had passed away, hence the name. I have to admit that when our parents told us that they were acquiring a German Shepherd, I was more than a little timid. Until then the only German Shepherds I had heard of were military dogs like Rin Tin Tin or K-9s working for the police department. Freebie would make a good guard dog, the general of the yard, but would she act like a pet too?

However, Freebie turned my world around. The same dog who ripped the back pocket off an intruder's jeans was the one who came to lick my face when I fell down rollerblading in the driveway. She dealt death by whiplash to every snake that slithered into our yard and still made time to play with every pear that fell from the tree. And when it came time for Gypsy to give birth, Freebie was more ready than the humans. In fact, she was the one that let us know the puppies had arrived.

When I got up one morning, Mom said, "Melissa, don't go outside."

"Why?"

"Gypsy had her puppies last night, and Freebie brought me one of the ones that didn't make it. Melissa, she was so gentle. She carried the puppy to me in her mouth and laid it at my feet. There isn't one tooth mark on its body."

"Oh my gosh!"

"I know. She then led me to two more of them lying in the yard. Let me check on Gypsy first and make sure there are no more dead puppies outside, and then you can come see them."

Dogs will naturally separate the live puppies from the dead ones, and in large litters, these deaths are quite common. But that a dog who is not the mother would be shaken by these deaths was something we did not expect. And after she had shown Mom where each dead puppy was, Freebie set to work with the seven survivors.

For us humans, puppy duty consisted of building a good pen to protect the mother and her little ones. Freebie may not have helped with that part of the work, but she made sure that pen was an extension of her yard. The puppies were not intruders; they were her nieces and nephews, and she was going to make sure that no snakes, raccoons, opossums, coyotes, or restless neighborhood boys would give them trouble. When they whined, she was at their sides. When they scrambled over the walls of the pen, she picked them up gently by the scruff of their necks and plopped them back inside. If one made a jail break, she was hot on its trail. And when my dad let them outside the pen to play, she made sure none slipped into the street. Except for the runt, which my sister had to feed with a bottle, there was hardly any work left for us to do.

However, the best part was mealtime, even with the poor little runt! Freebie had been neglected before the veterinarian had found her, so she really loved food. When Dad went to the food container, the guard dog turned into a little puppy herself and started yipping. Mom and Dad said she was singing for her supper. Well, when it was time for her meal, Freebie figured that the puppies needed to learn to sing too. She not only started the chorus, but she went from puppy to puppy to make sure they did their part before she went to her own bowl. I have no doubt the neighbors could have set their watches by Freebie and Gypsy's little band.

It did not take long before the puppies were grown, and all but two found homes, but still every night when Dad came outside, Freebie ran to Gypsy, then to each puppy, and finally to her bowl. Freebie also taught them how to defend their yard and even how to play what I like to call "shake a snake." But one day, we learned that Freebie had come down with congestive heart failure, and in a few weeks, she quietly passed away. That was the first time in seven years that mealtime was silent, and those puppies never sang for their supper again as long as they lived.

In the Cajun culture in which I was raised, a "nanny" is not an au pair. It is the name we call our godmothers, because they are deeply involved in our lives. That is precisely what Freebie was to those puppies and to our house. Personally, if I am ever blessed with a German Shepherd of my own, I hope it too keeps away the bad snakes but still finds time to lick away my tears and sing for its supper!

~Melissa Abraham

Take the First Step

The soul is the same in all living creatures,
although the body of each is different.
~Hippocrates

Thirty years ago, we lived in Edwardsville, Illinois, a small town that charmed us with friendly neighbors, a library that closed promptly at six, and Sunday concerts at the bandstand during the summer. It was a little bit of country, and we liked it.

Our best friends were Annie and Ted Zulmer, a young couple who had four rambunctious kids, all under the age of eight. They lived a few towns over, deeper in the country, so a visit usually meant packing sleeping bags and staying overnight.

Our baby, Lacey, usually clung to me or defended her playpen by throwing toys at any wannabe intruders. Her large, brown eyes viewed our friends' chaotic world suspiciously, especially their dog Max.

Max was a mutt, but once upon a time he'd earned respect as a hunting dog. He was retired now and acted like a grumpy old guy, sleeping in the sun and avoiding the kids. He didn't have the patience for squealing voices or small hands stroking his fur. He didn't bite or snap, just wiggled away if they got too close.

One April Saturday, when the crocuses finally popped out and summer seemed right around the corner, we were enjoying a lazy morning. The kids were watching cartoons in the playroom and the men were outside chopping wood. Annie and I were laughing at my efforts to knit. Nine-month-old Lacey sprawled on a blanket at my feet, playing with building blocks and her dolls.

As my stitches hopelessly tangled, Annie whispered, "Karla, don't panic, but look."

I looked. Lacey had crawled across the room, pushing toys out of her way. She grabbed a handful of Max's fur, struggling to stand up. I edged over quietly, not wanting him to wake up and maybe knock over my baby girl.

His eyes opened. I dropped to my knees, ready to grab her, a silent prayer in my heart. Max wasn't a mean dog and even now, his relaxed body was reassuring.

Somehow, it was okay.

The dog and baby stared at each other for what seemed to be an endless moment. Then, he nudged her, gently, as he would a young pup.

Lacey wavered to her knees, then her legs. Her balance was shaky and she broke into a babble of baby talk.

He stood up slowly and took a step.

She plopped back on her bottom. Her lips quivered. The springy carpet had cushioned her fall, so her wail was pure frustration.

He lay back down and nudged her again.

"I don't even believe this." Annie knelt by my side. "He's helping her. Kids, look."

We all stood transfixed as Max coaxed Lacey to stand. It took several tries, but finally she was successful.

He stepped forward, then swung his head around to peer into her face. Neither the animal or the baby could understand each other, but communication passed between them. His paternal instincts, long dormant, had kicked in. She sensed that he was an ally, able to calm her fears.

Though the old dog could no longer hunt, he could teach. He wanted Lacey to take that first step.

We all did.

Max stepped forward, slow and easy.

Lacey followed him, clutching his coat.

He took another.

Bouncing slightly on her feet and smiling, Lacey took another step.

They managed three steps before she fell into my arms. I hugged her, laughing as she described her wonderful experience in adorable baby talk. I joined the circle petting the old dog, his head lifted as proudly as any father.

"Good boy."

That weekend, we marveled as they repeated the performance. By the time my family left, Lacey was standing and taking a few steps alone.

All it had taken was an old hunting dog, past his prime, but full of heart.

Max never taught another baby to walk, but I told him that one day I'd tell his story as a special thank you.

So, I did.

~Karla Brown

Meet Our Contributors

Melissa Abraham resides with her husband in south Louisiana. She is a freelance translator specializing in French, Spanish, and Italian. She is the Newsletter Editor for the Writers' Guild of Acadiana and is currently working on a young adult fantasy novel. Follow her blog at www.melissaabraham.com.

Diane Ganzer Baum has been writing professionally since 2004. *Patrick the Wayward Setter* was her first published book, followed by many more for readers of all ages, both fiction as well as nonfiction. She is married and lives in a little town on the prairie in western Minnesota, where she plans to keep writing and gardening.

Karla Brown lives in Philadelphia with her husband and cat. She loves to garden, swim, cook, read, pursue all things chocolate, and daydream. She hopes to become a novelist, as she also writes paranormal romantic suspense, YA and middle grade.

Carol Chiodo Fleischman's writing has appeared in books, newspapers, and a textbook. Her topics cover a wide range of everyday events. A recurring theme is life as a blind person, especially the joys and challenges of using a seeing-eye dog. Pelican Publishing has scheduled a release for a children's book about her guide dog, Nadine.

Joyce Laird is a freelance writer living in Southern California with her menagerie of animal companions. Her features have been published in many magazines, including *Cat Fancy*, *Grit*, *Mature Living*,

I Love Cats and *Vibrant Life*. She contributes regularly to *Woman's World* and to the Chicken Soup for the Soul anthologies.

Cathi LaMarche spends most of her day reveling in the written word as a composition teacher, college essay coach, and novelist. Her work has appeared in twenty-three anthologies. She lives in Missouri with her husband, two children, and three spoiled dogs.

Diana Lynn is a business owner and freelance writer in Washington State. This is her sixth story published by Chicken Soup for the Soul. She jokes often about how no one is safe in her world; anyone can end up in a story—even the dog. E-mail her at Diana@ recoveringdysfunctional.com.

Marya Morin is a freelance writer. Her stories and poems have appeared in publications such as *Woman's World* and Hallmark. Marya also penned a weekly humorous column for an online newsletter, and writes custom poetry on request. She lives in the country with her husband. E-mail her at Akushla514@hotmail.com.

Jacqueline Pearce writes fiction for children and teens, including *Dog House Blues* and *The Truth About Rats (and Dogs)*, both written for the British Columbia Society for the Prevention of Cruelty to Animals (BC SPCA) Kids Club. She and her family still feel the absence of their dog, Dylan, who died three years ago.

Marcia Rudoff is the author of *We Have Stories — A Handbook for Writing Your Memoirs*. She lives and teaches writing in Bainbridge Island, WA. Favorite free-time activities involve grandkids, travel, and writing for Chicken Soup for the Soul books.

Annabel Sheila grew up in Stephenville, a pretty little town on the west coast of Newfoundland. She now calls Moncton, New Brunswick home with the love of her life, Rick, two senior cats, and her little dog, Ziggy. E-mail her at annabelsheila@live.ca.

Meet Amy Newmark

Amy Newmark is the bestselling author, editor-in-chief, and publisher of the *Chicken Soup for the Soul* book series. Since 2008, she has published 140 new books, most of them national bestsellers in the U.S. and Canada, more than doubling the number of Chicken Soup for the Soul titles in print today. She is also the author of *Simply Happy*, a crash course in Chicken Soup for the Soul advice and wisdom that is filled with easy-to-implement, practical tips for having a better life.

Amy is credited with revitalizing the Chicken Soup for the Soul brand, which has been a publishing industry phenomenon since the first book came out in 1993. By compiling inspirational and aspirational true stories curated from ordinary people who have had extraordinary experiences, Amy has kept the twenty-four-year-old Chicken Soup for the Soul brand fresh and relevant.

Amy graduated *magna cum laude* from Harvard University where she majored in Portuguese and minored in French. She then embarked on a three-decade career as a Wall Street analyst, a hedge fund manager, and a corporate executive in the technology field. She is a Chartered Financial Analyst.

Her return to literary pursuits was inevitable, as her honors thesis in college involved traveling throughout Brazil's impoverished northeast region, collecting stories from regular people. She is delighted to have come full circle in her writing career — from collecting stories "from the people" in Brazil as a twenty-year-old to, three decades later, collecting stories "from the people" for Chicken Soup for the Soul.

When Amy and her husband Bill, the CEO of Chicken Soup for the Soul, are not working, they are visiting their four grown children.

Follow Amy on Twitter @amynewmark. Listen to her free daily podcast, The Chicken Soup for the Soul Podcast, at www.chickensoup.podbean.com, or find it on iTunes, the Podcasts app on iPhone, or on your favorite podcast app on other devices.

Changing lives one story at a time®
www.chickensoup.com

Ayrshire Monographs 28

Historic Prestwick
and its surroundings
A guide for visitors

Ayrshire Archæological and Natural History Society
in association with
Kyle and Carrick Civic Society

2003

*Travel, in the younger sort, is part of education;
in the elder, a part of experience.*

Francis Bacon (1561-1626)

Front cover: *Prestwick Cross*
by James McMaster
[Courtesy of South Ayrshire Council]

Back cover: *Bachelors' Club, Tarbolton*
by John Doig

ISBN 0 9542253 1 7

Printed by
The Cromwell Press Ltd
Trowbridge
Wiltshire